SARS

Titles in the Series

Understanding Diseases and Disorders

SARS

Gail B. Stewart

KIDHAVEN PRESS

An imprint of Thomson Gale, a part of The Thomson Corporation

THOMSON

GALE

Detroit • New York • San Francisco • San Diego • New Haven, Conn. • Waterville, Maine • London • Munich

LIBRARY OF CONGRESS CATALOGING-IN-PUBLICATION DATA

Stewart, Gail, 1949–
  SARS / by Gail B. Stewart.
    p. cm. — (Understanding diseases and disorders)
Summary: Describes SARS, how it is treated, and what is being done to prevent future outbreaks of the disease.
  Simultaneously published: San Diego, Calif. : Lucent Books, 2004 (Diseases and disorders series).
  Includes bibliographical references and index.
  ISBN 0-7377-2642-3 (hard cover : alk. paper)
  1. SARS (Disease)—Juvenile literature. I. Title. II. Series.
  RC776.S27S74 2004b
  616.2—dc22
 	
                                2004010122

Printed in the United States of America

Contents

Chapter One

A Mystery Illness

In the early months of 2003 the world learned of a new and deadly disease. The first cases appeared in China in November 2002. By the time doctors there realized that the illness was very contagious, it had spread to other parts of Asia and even to Toronto, Canada.

By June 2003 the disease had become a worldwide threat. It had killed more than six hundred people on six continents. Researchers called the disease "severe **acute** respiratory syndrome," or SARS, for short. Although it had a name, no one knew how to stop it.

Guessing Wrong

The first cases of SARS were seen in Guangdong Province in southern China. People who had SARS felt achy, as though they were coming down with a cold. The symptoms were not alarming, especially for November. That is a rainy, cool time in Guangdong, and many people get coughs and colds.

After several days, however, people complained that their aches and pains were not getting better. Also, they developed dry coughs and fevers. They had trouble breathing, too. Many went to a clinic or hospital, hoping that a doctor could help them.

The Guangdong doctors first thought the disease was pneumonia. Fever and cough are typical of that disease. Patients were given **antibiotics**, which are used to fight some forms of pneumonia. They were also told to rest. However, patients did not improve. In fact, their symptoms became worse. Many had so much trouble breathing that they had to be

In early 2003, a SARS patient is rushed to the emergency room in Taiwan.

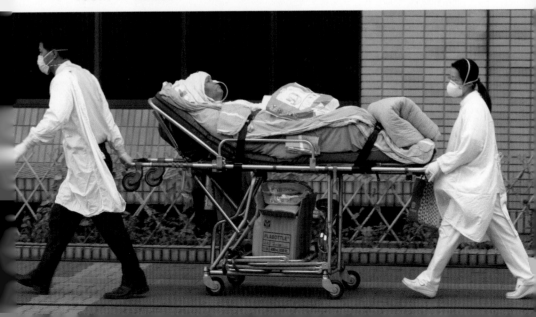

hooked up to special machines called **respirators**, to help them breathe.

From Bad to Worse

In the days that followed, some of the patients died. One nurse later said it was painful watching a patient with the disease try to breathe. She said it was like "watching a man drown to death on dry land."[1]

Doctors were baffled. They had never seen a respiratory disease that was so deadly and that did not respond to antibiotics. Doctors and nurses in Guangdong learned too late that unlike pneumonia, this disease was also contagious. Many health

Wearing surgical masks as protection from SARS, a group of women comforts a friend with an infected family member.

care workers, who had cared for patients without using face masks and gloves, became infected with the disease.

One nurse, for example, became ill after taking care of a patient with a dry cough and fever. At first she assumed that she was just tired from working hard or had caught the flu. Soon, however, the nurse was critically ill. "Breathing was difficult," she recalls, "and I had to be under a respirator for about ten days."[2] She was not the only one from her hospital to become ill. Ten other doctors, nurses, and orderlies were infected, too.

Recovery, the nurse says, has been slow. Even after a month, she was unable to work. "My lungs haven't got back to normal," she says, "and I still feel tight in my chest. . . . My muscles are so weak I can hardly lift anything, and my eyes are swollen and red."[3]

Keeping It Secret

People continued to get sick in Guangdong, and many died. Worried, doctors alerted local government officials about the spreading illness. They hoped radio and television stations would inform people of the problem and the symptoms.

However, the government in China was reluctant to spread the news of the disease. Government officials wanted to keep it secret. They felt that if people heard of a deadly disease that had no cure, they would lose faith in the government. Admitting

A doctor examines a woman for symptoms of SARS on a city street in Guangdong Province.

that they had a dangerous **epidemic** might also hurt China's economy. China depends on tourism and business from other countries. If people were afraid to go there for a vacation or business trip, China's economy would suffer.

For those reasons, Chinese officials kept the outbreak a secret. Because the government in China controls the radio and television stations, no announcements were made. This made it possible for the disease to spread further. Patients in Guangdong who were not getting well tried to get help at bigger hospitals in the province's capital city,

Guangzhou. However, doctors and nurses there had never seen this disease. They did not know how easily it spread. They did not use gloves or wear face masks when treating the new patients. In one hospital, a single patient infected more than twenty-six doctors and nurses.

Spreading Throughout the World

In February 2003 the event that doctors feared most happened. The disease spread beyond Guangdong Province. A doctor named Liu Jianlun went to Hong Kong for his nephew's wedding. Liu had not been feeling well, but he did not think he was seriously ill.

A hospital worker in Toronto, Canada, cleans a woman's hands before she puts on a surgical mask.

By the time he arrived at his hotel in Hong Kong, however, he felt terrible. He was coughing and had a fever. Liu realized that he might have SARS and went to the hospital in Hong Kong. He warned the emergency room staff to use masks and gloves when treating him. He did not want them to catch his disease.

His warnings were helpful. None of the doctors or nurses helping him became ill. However, a number of people at his hotel did get sick. Some of these people were from Hong Kong. Others were from faraway places including Canada, Vietnam, and Singapore. Without realizing it, Liu had infected people who would then spread the SARS germs to others.

What Can Be Done?

By April 2003 more than fifteen hundred people had become ill with SARS in Hong Kong. One large apartment building alone had 250 cases. In addition, the disease had become a danger in Toronto, Singapore, and Vietnam.

Each day brought more people to emergency rooms. Doctors and nurses were unsure of what to do. SARS had caught everyone by surprise, and there was no cure. One doctor in Toronto said that the hardest thing about SARS was how little they knew. "We're facing an enemy," he said, "that has no known shape, no identity, and no known effective treatment."[4]

Doctors pull a quarantined SARS victim into her room after she tried to jump out the window.

Doctors around the world watched helplessly as their patients gasped for breath and fought for their lives. Hospital staffs needed answers, and they needed them soon.

Chapter Two

Understanding SARS

China had instructed its doctors not to publicly discuss the epidemic. However, once it spread beyond China's borders, it could no longer be kept a secret. The World Health Organization, or WHO, issued a global alert on March 12, 2003.

WHO is an international public health agency. One of its jobs is to investigate dangerous new diseases that break out anywhere in the world. Once WHO officials are certain that a disease is a threat, the agency may issue warnings. Although the agency's information on SARS was sketchy, officials believed a very dangerous disease had become an international threat. Travelers were told to watch for symptoms such as a cough or fever. Emergency room staffs around the world were told to use masks and gloves when treating patients with these symptoms.

Identifying a Virus

Almost immediately, medical researchers began hunting for the cause of SARS and ways of treating or curing it. Doctors in China had already ruled out **bacteria** as the cause. Bacteria would have been visible under their microscopes. Also, antibiotics probably would have worked against a disease caused by bacteria.

A medical researcher prepares a culture of the SARS virus to study under a high-powered microscope.

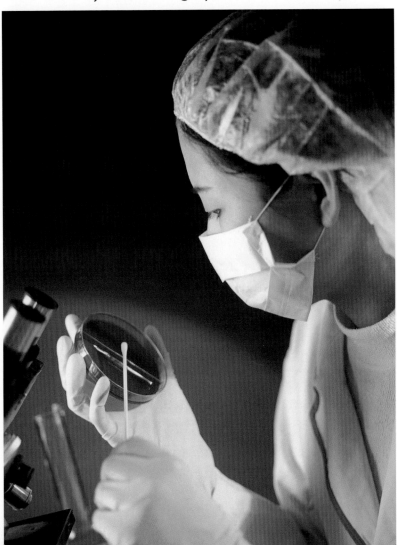

This led scientists to believe that a **virus** was to blame. Viruses are far more difficult to identify, however. Some are a million times smaller than bacteria. A virus can only be seen with a high-powered electron microscope, which can magnify objects over eighty thousand times. Scientists predicted that some form of flu virus would show up under the microscope.

As they looked at samples of blood and tissue from SARS patients with the electron microscope, however, they were surprised. Instead of a flu virus, they saw a coronavirus. Coronaviruses get their name from a Latin word *corona,* meaning "crown." The virus is round with crownlike spikes on its surface. One reporter who saw the virus under the microscope said that "magnified 100,000 times, [they] are fuzzy little balls that fill the screen and look like the burrs that stick to your pants during a hike in the woods."[5]

The presence of a coronavirus was puzzling. Doctors know that certain coronaviruses can make animals very sick. However, in humans, coronaviruses had never created serious problems. The most trouble a coronavirus had caused, as far as anyone knew, was the common cold. How could that virus be responsible for this deadly new disease?

Mutating

Researchers saw that the virus was similar to several other coronaviruses that infected animals. It was not exactly the same as any of them, howev-

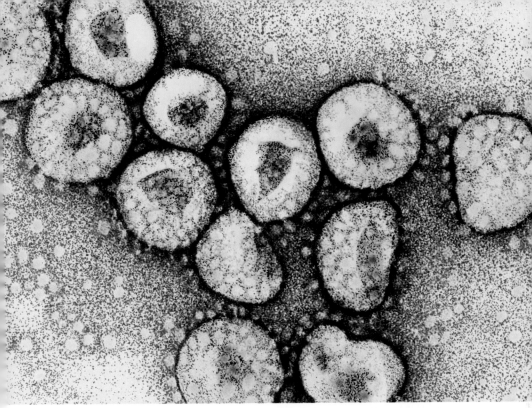

SARS is caused by a coronavirus (pictured), a round virus with crownlike spikes on its surface.

er. Whatever this virus was, it was something no one had ever seen before.

As scientists studied the virus, they saw that it behaved like other coronaviruses. Like all viruses, coronaviruses are unable to reproduce on their own. They can only survive by invading the cells of an animal. Once the virus invades the cell, it takes over. The virus uses the cell to duplicate itself over and over. Coronaviruses sometimes reproduce a thousand times in each cell. This process eventually kills the cells and the animal becomes sick.

Viruses that infect people differ from those that infect animals. That is why researchers speculated that a coronavirus harmful to animals had changed, or **mutated**. It looked as though, by mutating slightly, an animal coronavirus had become a deadly threat to people. But how did it happen?

The Wild Animal Markets

Scientists knew that the virus had begun in Guangdong Province, and they started their investigation there. They learned that the first cases of SARS were people who worked in animal markets in Guangdong. To determine whether these people could have been exposed to an animal virus, they visited some of the markets.

Animal markets are scattered throughout China, and there are many in Guangdong Province. Many Chinese people enjoy eating wild animals, not only for the taste, but because they believe eating certain animals can make them healthier. For instance, a long-tailed animal called a civet cat is said to help a person fight off disease. Giant salamanders are said to make a person's complexion smooth and wrinkle free.

At one Guangdong market, researchers saw hundreds of animal stalls. There were rows of cages balanced on top of one another, containing snakes, chickens, turtles, cats, frogs, and badgers. The cages were crowded and filthy. They reeked with the stink of blood and guts. Some of the animals were sick or dead. The researchers took samples of blood from some of the sickly animals in the market. They found the coronavirus in all of the animals

How the SARS Virus Is Transmitted from Animals to Humans

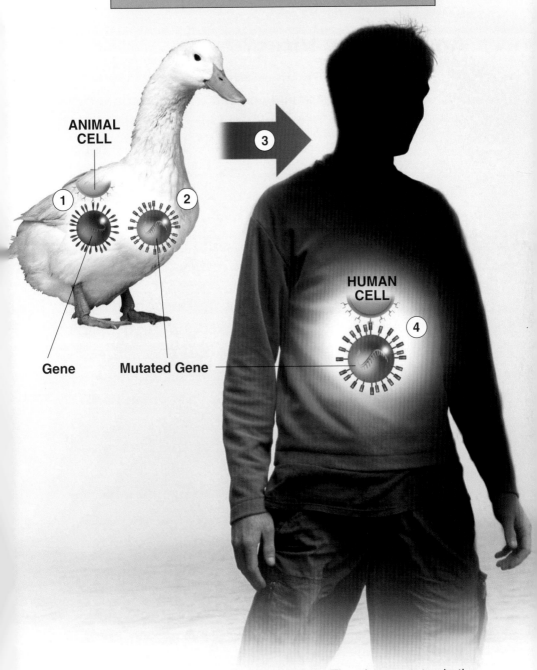

ANIMAL CELL

1

2

Gene

Mutated Gene

3

HUMAN CELL

4

An animal (1) is infected with the coronavirus. The virus mutates in the animal (2). The mutated virus is passed on (3) when a human handles the animal and comes in contact with the animal's blood. A human then becomes infected with the mutated coronavirus (4) and shows symptoms of SARS.

they tested. That indicated the SARS virus first made the animals sick.

An Airborne Virus?

It was not clear how the animal virus infected the humans. Some researchers felt that the virus could be airborne. It might have been inhaled by people as they worked in the crowded stalls. Other researchers were concerned that the workers did not wash their hands when butchering the animals. Perhaps a cut or scratch on their hands could have come in contact with blood from a sick animal.

Person to Person

Some researchers kept working on the connection between the animals in the market and the people. They wanted to find out how the virus jumped from one species to another. Other researchers concentrated on learning how SARS was spreading so quickly from person to person.

At first, scientists believed that the virus was spread only through close contact with a person infected with SARS. A person who accidently inhaled the spray from a SARS patient's sneeze or cough was thought to be at greatest risk. However, researchers were learning that the SARS virus could live for more than twenty-four hours outside the body. That suggested that the virus, left on a doorknob or elevator button by an infected person, could infect someone else who just touched that knob or button. This new information was disturbing, for it

A dance teacher and her students hold class for the first time since a SARS outbreak forced their Hong Kong school to close for two months.

showed that the virus was easier to catch than previously thought.

As the weeks went by, people around the world were becoming more frightened. There were more and more cases of SARS. Hundreds of people were dying from it. There was no medicine that could cure SARS patients, and no **vaccine** to prevent it. As emergency rooms struggled to treat new patients, doctors and researchers were at a loss for answers.

Chapter Three

Living with SARS

Without a vaccine to prevent SARS or a drug to cure it, people had to learn to be very careful. The best way to fight SARS was to keep it from spreading. Doctors learned that people who were exposed to SARS did not get sick right away. Often a week could go by before they got symptoms of the disease. That meant that people could have the virus and infect others without even knowing it.

"We Do What We Have to Do"

By February 2003 doctors had started separating, or isolating, SARS patients to keep the illness from spreading to other patients. However, health officials insisted that family members and friends of SARS patients be **quarantined**, or isolated, too. A person under quarantine could not go to school, to work, or even go outside to do an errand. Once ten days had gone by and the person had not become ill, the quarantine was lifted.

Many nations, especially in Asia, made strict rules about travelers, too. They wanted to make sure that no new cases of SARS came across their borders. At the airport in Singapore, travelers getting off planes were greeted by nurses. Every new arrival was screened by special scanners that would beep if a person had a fever. Anyone who set off the beeper was quickly taken to a quarantine center.

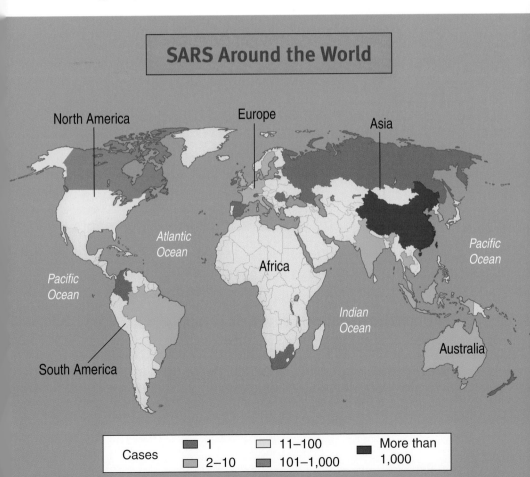

SARS Around the World

Anyone who resisted or complained about being quarantined was fitted with an electronic wristband. The wristband would go off if the person tried to leave the quarantine center. People trying to escape had to pay fines of five thousand dollars and were jailed for six months after the two-week quarantine was completed.

The minister of health in Singapore explained that they had to be serious about SARS. One new case, he said, could start a new explosion of cases in Singapore. "We do what we have to do," he said in March 2003. "I don't think we've seen anything like this before, and it is a global problem. For now, this is a battle that is being fought with the thermometer and quarantine."[6]

Afraid

In China, life changed very quickly. When government officials understood that they had a massive outbreak on their hands, they laid down rules to keep the disease from spreading any further.

Every four hours public service announcements were broadcast on the radio. These announcements urged people to wash their hands and wear face masks when in public places. The government enlisted volunteers to stand on street corners and take people's temperatures. There was even a rule that people had to spray disinfectant on their bicycle and automobile tires. That way, any germs from the streets would be killed before they could do more damage.

People traveling within China were often given checkups before being allowed to board trains. At the height of the SARS scare in China one young man took a fourteen-hour train trip from Beijing to his hometown. He received a physical before being allowed to board the train. In addition, railroad workers came to his section of the train several times during the trip to spray disinfectant.

Reminders Everywhere

In China and other Asian countries daily life changed for everyone. Everywhere, it seemed, there were reminders of the SARS threat. Children were

Young men play video games in a Hong Kong arcade despite the high risk of exposure to the SARS virus.

affected, because the government canceled schools. Preschools, day care services, and babysitters were told to close their doors, too. That affected many parents who had jobs during the day.

Officials urged zoos, museums, playgrounds, and shopping centers to close. One mother says that it was hard on children celebrating their birthdays. She had to cancel her young daughter's party because many of the children had left the city with their parents.

Churchgoers were affected, too. Catholic churches in some Asian countries canceled confession. Instead, the churches made a general message of forgiveness that applied to everyone. In some churches, communion was not offered and people were told not to dip their hands in holy water.

Masks and More Masks

Face masks were the most obvious reminder of SARS. The masks commonly sold in stores were not constructed to keep out tiny viruses as were those worn by hospital workers. Even so, people were urged by health officials to keep a mask on whenever they were outside. Stores selling face masks were crowded with people. However, the supplies ran out quickly. Some store owners said that customers fought one another to get the last mask on the shelf.

There were even colorful face masks that appealed to children. On street corners in Singapore, merchants sold masks in turquoise, red, pink, or orange. Some

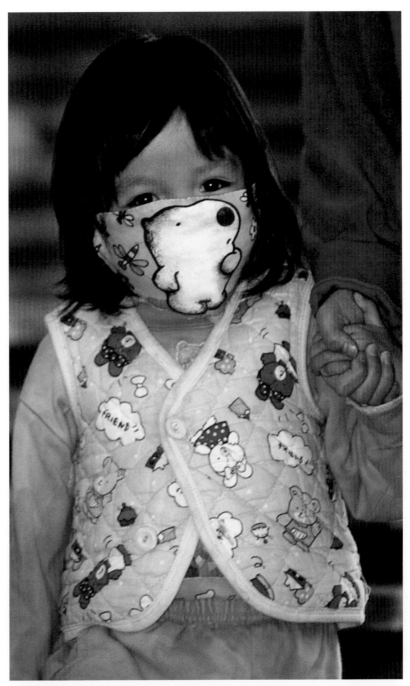

A young Chinese girl wears a protective mask with a colorful cartoon character printed on it.

had pictures of Disney characters such as Bambi or the Little Mermaid. These were bought by parents whose small children would not wear their face masks. One mother said her children would not wear the plain masks, but she thought they would like the Bambi masks. "With cartoons on them," she said, "they might change their minds."[7]

Paul, who was in Hong Kong during the SARS epidemic, says that even on television, people wore masks. "The news guys, the weather reporter—everybody," he says. "And on talk shows, everyone sat around a table wearing masks. One young Chinese singer was on a show, and she sang with her mask on."[8]

Doctors and Nurses

The SARS epidemic had a particularly great impact on medical workers. In areas where there were many cases of SARS, doctors and nurses were most at risk. In the early weeks of the disease in China, Hong Kong, Vietnam, and Toronto, medical workers were infected with SARS more than any other group.

As doctors and nurses became ill, there was a shortage of hospital workers. Those who did not get SARS often had to work extra shifts. They became tired and discouraged. "They're not getting enough sleep, [and] they struggle with putting on their protective gear," said one supervisor in a Toronto hospital, "and they are worried about getting infected themselves."[9]

Many doctors and nurses said it made them nervous to be around patients with coughs or fevers. They wanted to do their jobs, but they were afraid. One visiting doctor to a Toronto hospital noticed that a lot of doctors refused to take off their face masks and protective gowns when they were in the staff lounges. "It was eerie," said the visiting doctor, "like you were on Mars or on a new planet. You sit in meetings, everyone around the table is wearing [a] mask."[10]

A Hong Kong restaurant worker protects herself from SARS as her customers eat without masks.

Difficult Funerals

The epidemic created problems for families of SARS victims, too. It is traditional in China for people to stay with dying family members, keeping a vigil. It is considered very important for a dying person to spend his or her last moments with loved ones.

However, when doctors in China and Hong Kong realized how contagious SARS was, they did not want family members in the same room. By April 2003 hospitals had rules preventing any visits by family members to SARS patients.

During the funeral of a nurse who died of SARS, the coffin is kept closed to help contain the virus.

Problems for families planning funerals arose, too. Funeral directors were worried that the dead body might spread SARS to funeral goers. Although Asian funerals are almost always held with an open casket, the threat of SARS changed that.

Even with such changes, however, funerals tended to be small. Many people were worried about becoming infected, even with the casket closed. As a result, the families of SARS victims had less support from friends. That made a very hard time even worse for them. It seemed that even after a death, SARS continued to cause problems.

Chapter Four

What Next?

Though the situation seemed bleak in the spring of 2003, by July of that year there was good news. The World Health Organization announced that SARS had been contained. There were still people suffering from the disease, but they had been isolated. No new cases had been reported, and health officials were hoping for the best.

There were still concerns about SARS, however. Because SARS is a coronavirus, like the common cold, some doctors felt it could be seasonal. Perhaps when the winter cold season returned, SARS would make a comeback. Many health officials agreed that although there were no new cases of SARS, the virus was still a threat. One new case, they said, was all it would take for a new outbreak to occur. Dr. David Heymann of WHO warned, "It's very important countries continue their **surveillance** [watchfulness] for at least the next twelve months."[11]

A New Outbreak

In the spring of 2004 health officials' fears came true. On April 25, 2004, doctors in China announced that

A Chinese woman suspected of having SARS arrives at a hospital in Guangdong Province in January 2004.

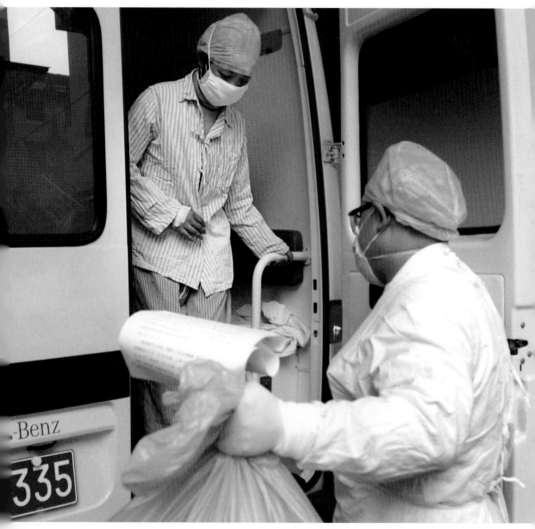

-Benz

335

there were four new cases of SARS in their country. Doctors believe that the first new victim was a twenty-six-year-old graduate student named Song, who worked in a medical laboratory. In that laboratory, researchers study a number of dangerous viruses, including the SARS virus.

According to Chinese health officials, Song became ill on March 25, 2004, with what she thought was pneumonia. She did not even suspect her illness could have been caused by the SARS virus. Song traveled by train to a hospital to receive treatment for her illness. She was released from the hospital, with no

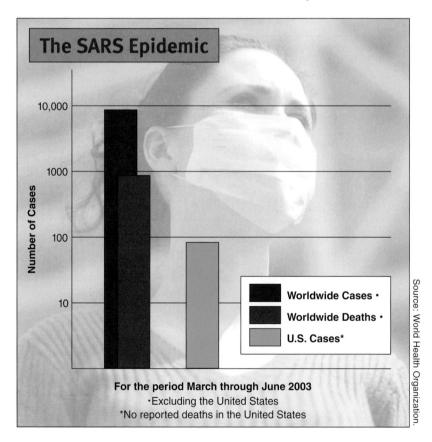

The SARS Epidemic

Number of Cases

10,000

1000

100

10

Worldwide Cases ·
Worldwide Deaths ·
U.S. Cases*

For the period March through June 2003
·Excluding the United States
*No reported deaths in the United States

Source: World Health Organization.

one suspecting SARS. Her mother, who was taking care of her, became ill soon afterward. After her mother died, on April 19, officials realized they were dealing with a SARS outbreak. By then two more people, including one hospital worker, had developed SARS.

China Responds Quickly

Officials in China were very worried that there would be even more victims. Song had traveled by train on three occasions before she knew she was sick. That meant she almost certainly had infected other people before she understood that she had SARS. Health officials made lists of places where Song and her mother might have exposed others to the SARS virus.

Once they knew it was SARS, the Chinese government acted quickly. National health officials announced a quarantine that they hoped would stop the spread of the virus. Almost five hundred people who were known to have come in contact with Song, her mother, or the other two SARS cases were isolated. China's quick response may have helped keep this new outbreak from growing out of control.

Even so, some SARS experts were perplexed. Why did a research worker who works with viruses not take precautions once she became ill? And if she did not make the connection between her illness and SARS, why did the doctors who treated her not make

Quarantined students at Beijing University do morning exercises in early 2004.

that connection? One researcher says that an illness similar to pneumonia in any medical worker "should have been a very big red flag."[12]

A Possible Cure

The recent oubreak of SARS reminds doctors that the disease could again spread beyond China's borders. SARS is still a threat. For that reason, researchers have been working hard to find either a cure or a vaccine. At the University of Massachusetts Medical School, scientists have had some success. They have been trying to produce **antibodies**, which the body normally makes as it fights an infection. If scientists could make antibodies to fight SARS, they could inject them into patients to help fight the virus.

In April 2004 researchers were hopeful that they were on the right track. One of the Massachusetts researchers said she and her colleagues were well aware of the need to work quickly. "When faced with an outbreak of a deadly infectious disease like SARS," she said, "[people in public health] need to move fast."[13] Chinese laboratories were planning to begin testing the man-made antibodies soon. However, experts stressed that testing could take at least two years before the drug was available to everyone.

Students in Hong Kong take each other's temperature during the 2004 SARS outbreak.

Problems Ahead

Progress toward a cure is good news. However, scientists say that there still may be problems ahead. Some of the practices that led to SARS continue.

Officials in China have warned people about the animal markets. They have made it illegal to buy or sell wild animals for food. However, the animal markets are still in business.

One reporter went back to Guangdong Province after the new law was enacted. He wrote that the sellers are still there, but that they are more careful. If a health inspector is nearby, they take their cages and disappear. Because of the added risks from inspectors, many market workers are charging more for the animals they sell. Even though the price has increased, however, people are willing to pay.

One Hong Kong researcher has proposed a solution to the problem. He says that certain wild animals could be raised on farms. They could be monitored for germs and disease. The slaughterhouses, too, could be checked for cleanliness. That system might avoid the filthy conditions of the markets where so many sick animals are butchered.

Next Time

The SARS epidemic taught scientists a great many things. They learned that a virus can jump from animals to humans with deadly consequences. They also learned how in the age of international airline travel, a virus in a remote part of China can quickly become a

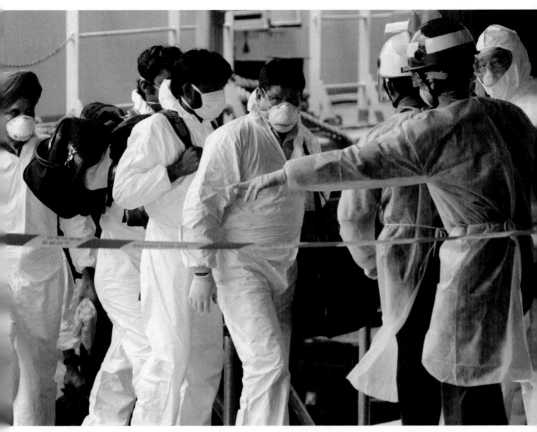

Hong Kong health officials quarantine a group of sailors from India who showed symptoms of SARS.

worldwide threat. If another outbreak of SARS occurs—or when the next dangerous new virus appears—it will almost certainly be a global problem.

Wherever the next outbreak of a new disease strikes, doctors need to alert WHO and other health agencies. What are the symptoms of the disease? How does it spread? By sharing information with doctors and hospitals around the world, they may be able to stop the virus's spread before it is out of control.

Notes

Chapter 1: A Mystery Illness

1. Quoted in James Kelly, "Making News on the SARS Front," *Time,* May 5, 2003, p. 8.
2. Quoted in BBC News, "Eyewitness: Vietnam's SARS Survivor," April 17, 2003. www.news.bbc.co.uk.
3. Quoted in BBC News, "Eyewitness."
4. Quoted in Hannah Beech, "Doing Battle with the Bug," *Time International,* April 14, 2003, p. 44.

Chapter 2: Understanding SARS

5. Michael Lemonick, "Will SARS Strike Here?" *Time,* April 14, 2003, p. 72.

Chapter 3: Living with SARS

6. Quoted in Elizabeth Rosenthal, "From China's Provinces, a Crafty Germ Spreads," *New York Times,* April 27, 2003, p. A3.
7. Quoted in Matt Mottinger and Rebecca Buckman, "Holding Their Breath," *Wall Street Journal,* March 28, 2003, p. A1.
8. Paul, telephone interview, September 1, 2003.

9. Quoted in Lawrence Altman, "Behind the Mask, the Fear of SARS," *New York Times,* June 24, 2003, p. F1.
10. Quoted in Altman, "Behind the Mask," p. F1.

Chapter 4: What Next?

11. Quoted in Keith Bradsher, "SARS Declared Contained, with No Cases in Past 20 Days," *New York Times,* July 6, 2003.
12. Quoted in Susan Jakes, "SARS Returns to China," *Time Asia,* May 3, 2004. www.time.com/time/asia/magazine/printout/0,13675,5010.
13. Quoted in "SARS Treatment Developed at UMass Medical School to Be Tested by Chinese Biotech Firm," *Mass High Tech,* April 26, 2004. www.masshightech.com/displayarticledetail.asp?Art_ID=65524.

Glossary

acute: Intense or severe.

antibiotics: Drugs used to fight certain infections and diseases.

antibodies: Substances created by the body as it fights off a disease.

bacteria: Microscopic organisms that can cause infections and disease.

epidemic: A widespread outbreak of a disease in a certain region.

mutate: Change slightly. The SARS virus is believed to have mutated from a virus that infected only animals.

quarantine: The forced isolation of a person with a disease or who has been exposed to a disease.

respirator: A machine that helps a person breathe.

surveillance: Watchfulness.

vaccine: A drug that can prevent a person from becoming infected with a disease.

virus: A cause of some diseases. Viruses are far smaller than bacteria and cannot be fought with antibiotics.

For Further Exploration

Books

Mark P. Friedlander, *Outbreak: Disease Detectives at Work.* Minneapolis: Lerner, 2003. Very good information about the methods researchers use to study a new disease. Also contains a helpful section on how viruses can be used by terrorists.

P.C. Leung and E.E. Ooi, eds., *SARS War: Combatting the Disease.* Singapore: World Scientific, 2003. This has some good background on various viruses and diseases in China.

Fred Ramen, *Influenza.* New York: Rosen, 2001. A very readable book, with a good section on one of the most deadly viruses in history—the 1918 influenza virus.

Periodicals

Denise Grady and Lawrence Altman, "Rise of a Virus: Cracking the Mystery," *New York Times,* May 26, 2003.

Susan Jakes, "SARS Returns to China," *Time Asia,* May 3, 2004.

Web Sites

CDC (www.cdc.gov). This is the official Web site of the Centers for Disease Control and Prevention. The CDC had an important role in researching the SARS virus, and the Web site contains good information about the spread of the disease.

World Health Organization (www.who.int). WHO's site has up-to-the-minute articles and bulletins about any SARS news around the world.

Index

Picture Credits

About the Author

Gail B. Stewart received her undergraduate degree from Gustavus Adolphus College in St. Peter, Minnesota. She did her graduate work in English, linguistics, and curriculum study at the College of St. Thomas and the University of Minnesota. She taught English and reading for more than ten years.

She has written over ninety books for young people, including a series for Lucent Books called The Other America. She has written many books on historical topics such as World War I and the Warsaw ghetto.

Stewart and her husband live in Minneapolis with their three sons, Ted, Elliot, and Flynn; two dogs; and a cat. When she is not writing, she enjoys reading, walking, and watching her sons play soccer.